The Dream Catcher Food for Thought

Antione Denzel Lacey

Editor: Bea Gyimah

ISBN: **0692728023**
ISBN-13: 978-0692728024

If there is not an audience chanting in your name, be the audience. Be inspired by your own creativity and shine brighter than any diamond pulled from Earth.

– Antione D. Lacey

CONTENTS

Chapter Five: My Protest Against Social Injustices

Chapter Six: My Inner Strength

Chapter Seven: My Identity

Chapter Eight: Power Of Faith

PRAYER OF MINES

God every day I just want to thank you. Thank you for blessing me with the people in my life that are close to my heart. You always helped me throughout my life, showing me the way to your kingdom. My life has been a little rocky, but you continue to help me through it all. God, always be in my heart and on my mind. Help me to be a wiser person and to help anyone in need. I want to love those who hate so much. With your help, I want to become a person who brings joy to those who are sad. With your help God, I need your guidance to make good decisions in my life. With you, anything is possible. God bless anyone who is reading this and keep them in good health and good spirits.

God, Thank you.
In Jesus name, Amen

My

Romance

Patience

Patience is,

Looking at the one you love.

Admiring her looks…

And the way she moves.

Patience is,

Looking into her beautiful brown eyes,

Blinded by heaven's gifts.

The words she speaks,

Flow like a melody from the soul.

Patience is,

It's the way her love caresses the soul,

When it's sad and lonesome.

It's the touch of her holding your body,

Comforting your heart.

Patience is,

Seeing her true side.

Allowing her to show her emotions,

Going through trials and tribulations.

Patience is,

Giving her an unexpected gift.

Having crazy moments,

To see her smile and laugh.

It's showing her eternal love.

Casual Thinking

In the optimistic corners

Of my room,

I think of *you*.

Looking into a reflection,

I see *you*.

As if you're looking at me

Looking at you.

Driving myself crazy

Craving to be around *you*.

You are my crazy obsession.

Teaching me lessons

About the essence

Of a blessing.

Dabbles of hearts,

Going across pages of my notebook.

Saying how much "I love you,"

But, this insanity is *love*.

Mindful Questioning

Venting,

Through my thoughts.

All I do is wonder when.

When shall I see you.

Being able to caress

A kiss upon your face.

Wrapping my arms

Around your waist.

Allowing our souls to intertwine.

To be in love

With your mind,

Interlocked with your thoughts.

Not departing our time.

But again,

I just wonder when.

Only time will tell.

Mind within the Clouds

It's been times when I stared at the moon.

Wondering,

If our view was the same.

Mesmerized by the sky,

That sits above me.

If I could,

I would reach my hands,

Over the distance between us.

Just to hold you in my arms.

I would ask God to rearrange the stars,

In the message spelled out for you.

Yelling to the heavens,

To make my voice…

Echo so *you* would hear it.

Passionate Musing on My Muse

Wet Dream

In my dreams,

I kiss pink lips

Of her divine mind.

Penetrating her thoughts,

Spreading her canvas.

Painting a perfect picture,

With every stroke.

Our hearts beating as one.

Her quivering body,

Lying between the silk sheets.

Her sweet touch caresses my soul,

Sending chills through my body.

A sudden wake and it's just a blur.

Blasphemy when my mind thinks unnaturally.

Looking at my bed like it's a dream,

Because it has to be.

Only way I can see my beauty to be,

Is going back to sleep.

4 Roses

The Passionate fire igniting between us.

Establishing the bond within our hearts.

Intertwining our souls with faith,

From the man above.

Creating a foundation of love

With one another.

Forbidden Fruit

Her fragrant scent entices me.

I suckle her lips with passion.

The taste of her sweet nectar quenches my tongue.

Kissing her tender juices.

A delightful smile hinders my face.

The fruits of her labor,

Become my joy...

And her *pleasure*.

My Heartache, Loss, & Regret

Anxiety

As I look at the glass,

I wonder if you miss me.

Scrolling through our conversations,

Feeling the beating in my chest.

As I look at the glass,

I wonder do you *love* me?

Constantly scrolling,

Adding more questions to my thoughts.

Looking beyond this glass,

My *vision* is not clear.

I think of us.

Only seeing the sight of what my heart feels.

As I look at the glass,

At times I think,

I'm smothering you with my emotions.

Emotions I kept bottled up,

Erupting into an uncontrollable rage.

As I look at the glass,

It breaks.

What is Love?

A cultivating illusion,

Used to poison a fragile soul.

Denying all signs of hurt,

Just to feel something.

What is love?

Looking past false reality,

Drowning in your thoughts.

To physically feel an existence,

That wasn't there to begin with.

March 5th (Ballet Recital)

Sorrow was her name.

Beautiful silver swan,

Who used my skin as her stage.

Dancing slowly,

Until the stage turn red.

The audience of bottles,

Clapped in her name.

Throwing bouquet of roses,

Leaving scars of depression

Upon my skin.

She danced once more,

Until the music stopped.

Giving me a sense of hope,

But, the music began again.

The beautiful swan

Altered my body.

Play Toy

She used me like stationary tissues.

Wiping away her tears,

As it climaxed on her face.

Embraced her mistakes,

Erasing it with laugher.

A pawn in her childish game.

Like contacts,

Our vision was clear.

Now,

I'm just a disposable.

An inanimate object,

She uses from time to time.

Twisting my ligaments,

Until pain disburses

Throughout my body.

Crippling my heart,

Corrupting me with fear.

To love,

Caring for someone else.

Reminisce

I miss you.

Missing the person,

Of which you were.

Now those memories,

Linger like shadows.

Encrypting its way in my thoughts.

Remembrance of you.

Your name still utters the bows

Of my tongue.

Kissing the nakedness of my lips.

When you left,

So did the four letters.

L.O.V.E.

My Rose

Your beauty is the essence

Of which I neglected.

And for that,

I am sorry.

Sorry,

To not water

Your roots with my love.

I miss your grace

Within my presence.

I missed showering

Your petals with my attention.

Forgot to trim your buds,

When you bruised them.

You showed me love.

I looked away,

Due to the past flowers,

Stabbing my hands.

Now,

Your crimson body

Lays still within my lap.

Vices & My
Inner Struggles

The Visit (meeting with the Voodoo lady)

She said,

What will satisfy your hunger?

To devour all my nightmares,

Until I no longer know

The word *fear.*

To not quiver in my skin,

As it holds a gun to my face.

Having the satisfaction

Of happiness,

Even though I've lost my patience.

Having the world

Beneath my feet.

And not digging within

The emptiness of my pockets,

Help me feast.

Undoing my wrongs

And purge my sins.

Darkest Hour

The yellow moon

Sits over my view of discomfort

Memories and broken promises.

It reflects upon the written words

Of lies and confusion.

As I drink from it,

It becomes my poison

And I its *victim*.

Veronica (My Poison)

She goes by many names,

Mango, strawberry, and acid drop.

She's my poison.

Even though she makes me sick,

Her love is intoxicating.

The potent mixture

Of fornication.

As I gulped her sweet mellow scent,

Purging my sins

Once more.

Turning my pure soul

Into a helpless fiend.

Waking up with the taste of her

On my tongue,

And a headache.

Waiting and wishing,

To be in the essence…

Of Veronica again.

Laughter

Laughter is like a drug,

Used to change a disfigured image.

We laugh to disguise the pain

That still grows inside.

We laugh to hold back familiar tears

That taste like grains of salt.

We laugh to take away,

What we thought existed

But, was just an illusion.

Wanda (My Nightmare)

Heavy influence

On the minds of the weak.

Essence,

Of sin that is evil.

Unholy,

Impure goddess reeking of death.

When questioned, I answer.

Invoking my presence

Within the ganja smoke.

Inhaling her in my lungs,

We are *one*.

Corrupted I become,

I slowly fall victim to *Wanda*.

Her Story

I was the witness to her pain.

On lonely nights,

She wept rivers of depression.

Positive attention became negative scars.

Nursed her war wounds,

Using her temple as an obscene object.

Money became monogamous,

On the figure she gains.

Snoring lines of her dreams,

To ease the pain.

What it's worth,

She said the satisfaction she never had.

Her beauty remained still,

As her body kissed the floor.

Reasons of her death weren't televised.

People believed the lies,

Her family told.

Never looked into her eyes,

And seen what her windows behold.

Hallucination

Pretending to be a part of a nonexistence.

They say they "love you,"

But your name not even mention.

Running through the motions

Of the mind being twisted.

Is this the life,

Or a reality of straight fiction.

Cultivating thoughts,

Causing mental afflictions.

Minor addictions,

Turning into sleepless nights.

Fighting with my thoughts,

Chasing them with cracked bottles.

There are a lot of bottles,

Filled with pain and heartbreak.

My Protest Against Social Injustice

It Hurts

It *hurts*

To see burning flesh,

Of my flesh, of my people.

Displayed on Medias' silver screen.

It *hurts*

Feeling my ancestors sorrows,

Through the dry winds

And blood soaked soil.

Hearing the violence of *mankind.*

Misery beating on the door,

With guns and pitchforks.

It *hurts*

Speaking words of love,

When it's only used for lust.

Lusting over one's body,

Instead of one's mind.

It *hurts*

Seeing bottles and shell cases

Hit the ground,

Kissing the cold payment.

Another one of my brothers

Or sisters caressed death's lips.

Babylon

Bones of my ancestors,

It was built on.

Streets paved with blood,

Reeking of foul smells.

Crying shadows screaming for justice,

But, they only hear silence.

Educated minds…

Lacking a sense of knowledge.

Trading their beliefs,

For an unrealistic profit.

Rappers call themselves "poets,"

But, only speak of violence.

Children casting out Bibles,

Pushing daisies…

With unholy rifles.

My brothers rot behind the bars

Of injustice and criminalization.

Some say it's heaven on earth,

But, it's just hell waiting.

Two Cities

The city streets

Filter the night sky.

Cascading over shades of grey,

It holds within its bosom.

By day,

The street lights stay dim

With the cities depression.

Regurgitating the problems and hardships

Of its people.

When the night falls,

The city bloom with bouquets of lights.

Filling the city with life,

To bask in its hope once more.

Belief and Forgiveness

They believed *you*

When *you* cascaded images

Of *my* people.

Rioting the streets like animals.

She forgave *you*,

When *you* bought her forgiveness

For killing her son.

They believe *you*,

When *you* ruled my sister's death

As a suicide.

We forgave *you*,

When *you* sentenced the officer,

But, her death still unjustified.

They believed *you*.

When *you* told us

The unholy pyrite water

Was good to drink.

We forgave *you*,

When **They** gave *us* water

Still,

You deprived *our* youth.

Our forgiveness,

Shall not be in vain.

Nor,

Shall they believe *your* lies.

My Inner Strength

Determined

They looked at me like a monster,

And didn't understand my greatness.

When I was pushing my potential,

They were trying my patience.

They laughed behind my back,

And fooled me with lies.

Never knew the pain they caused,

When they looked in my eyes.

It's been times,

When I felt like

My life is at a standstill.

Walking through ditches,

And stepping on unholy landfills.

Wearing my heart on my sleeve,

With my dreams wrapped in rags.

When the structure of life...

Always come with a price tag.

See me, I'm just trying to be stable.

Educate myself...

And put food on the table.

Live a good life with Godly things in it.

Not worrying about the evils,

Knocking on the door to collect rent.

Imagine (Black Ice Resurrection)

Imagine

If false idols didn't push 360 deals

Telling you to use these hollow tips,

And stack these bills.

Instead of using a book,

Saying let's do this for real.

Imagine

If success was the only thing to steal.

So a bullet in the chamber

Isn't a reason to kill,

Unless for protection.

Don't lead by example,

If your audience are balloons

And will pop under pressure.

Dream Once More

Conqueror all harsh fears.

Pursuit the everlasting.

Run towards goals of life.

Where I'm From

I'm from

A city of success,

Clouded by toxic smoke.

Where being a statistic

Is the daily attire.

Chalk lines and caution tape,

Becomes your breakfast.

Where churches,

Bless the neighborhood corners.

Heartless soul's float

Like hollow shadows.

Street corners,

Become a junkie's kitchen sink.

Fiends,

Bask in the morning's sin.

Kissing hollow pipes,

Smoking their dreams away.

My home,

Where some blind fold success

And tape its mouth shut.

Insomnia

My dreams do not sleep.

So why should I?

Strength

Being strong,

Is defined as a means

Of staying alive.

We are strong

Dealing with the fears

Lying in the depths of our souls.

And if we shall cry,

Then,

The tears of joy will fall.

For even the strong,

Weep within their shadows.

My Identity

Black (who I am)

I *am…*

The beauty behind the scars

My ancestors took beatings to.

I *am…*

Inerasable,

But, traceable within my roots.

I *am…*

The color of nature,

Keeping us grounded.

I *am*,

The lion that walks

Through the concrete jungles.

But,

I am not the beast

Society portrays me as.

I *am*

A **Black** king,

Without the thorns.

My name shall echo

In deaf ears.

You Gone Get This Work

You say,

Being a real *Nigga* is an achievement,

And being an over achiever

Is an option.

Fooling the world

Just to make a simple profit.

If they only knew

You were a con artist.

Proclaiming you a vessel

For God,

Sinning in his name.

It's like the last supper

When you're in my presence.

If having dreams

Makes you starve.

Having money,

Makes you a target.

I would rather starve,

Than to eat

From your plate.

My victory shall come.

You will be eating

From the depth

Of my hands.

Momma Said

Momma *said*,

"Closed mouths don't get fed.

So your words

Shall not be bitten.

Nor hold your tongue,

That conceals ammunition."

Momma *said*,

"Don't let the *Devil* break you.

Put your faith

In God's hands.

You shall not—

Be *defeated*."

Momma *said*,

"You are a king.

Hold *your* head up high.

Place your crown

Of identity

Upon your head."

Momma *said*,

"I love you.

You are more than a dreamer."

Remember me

Remember me—

Like an unforgotten Memory.

Like the first time…

We kissed.

Remember me—

As a King.

Who rose from the cinder blocks,

Feasting upon

His ambitions.

Remember me—

As the Lion roaming…

The land.

Trying to find,

Peace within.

Forget me not,

As my body turns back

To sand.

Don't cry because

You won't *ever* forget me.

So, remember me.

The Power of My Faith

Rebirth

As I put my faith

In this *Bible*,

It mimics the shape

Of a bottle.

The day,

I found my salvation.

It comforts me,

When I am low.

Gives me life,

When I am empty.

With every word

Of the tongue,

My sins are abolished.

Drinking,

Until I am whole again.

God Speaks

You live to be happy,

And always stay humbled.

You may walk a long journey,

To fall and stumble.

Always rise to *your* feet,

And, keep your head sky high.

Some people will lie,

Others will decide your fate.

Show their justified smiles,

To conceal their hate.

Believe and have faith in me,

Receiving my blessings.

The world you see right now—

Is the *ultimate* lesson.

Heaven

Dreamt that I could fly.

Flew without hesitation.

Met God at the gate.